Zappity ZAP ZAP!
A Look at Electricity

Illustrations: Janet Moneymaker
Design/Editing: Marjie Bassler

Zappity ZAP ZAP! A Look at Electricity
ISBN 978-1-950415-25-0

Published by Gravitas Publications Inc.
www.gravitaspublications.com
www.realscience4kids.com

What happens when you rub a balloon in hair?

I do not know.

I will try it.

What happens when you touch a doorknob after rubbing your socks on the carpet?

What happens when you
turn on your toy plane?

What happens when
you plug in a toaster?

It works?

Sticky balloons, zapping doorknobs, flying planes, and hot toasters all use some type of **electricity**...

...to make hair fly,

...to shock your fingers,

...to make your toy airplane soar through the sky,

...and to toast your bread.

Electricity is a general term

for **electrical energy.**

Energy is needed to do **work.**

Work happens when a **force** moves an object.

Force is any action that changes...

...the **location** of an object,

...the **shape** of an object,

...**how fast or how slowly** an object is moving. (This is called the **speed** of an object.)

Electrical energy comes from **electrons,** which are a part of an atom.

Electrons are shown as arms in these drawings of atoms.

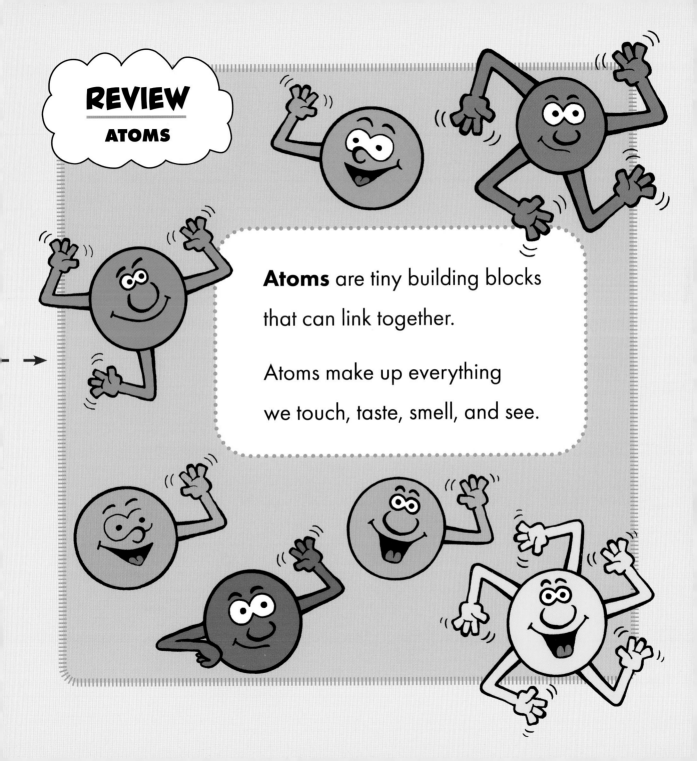

ATOMS

Atoms are tiny building blocks that can link together.

Atoms make up everything we touch, taste, smell, and see.

We can also draw electrons

by replacing the arms with dots.

Sometimes electrons hop
from atom to atom.

What happens
when they do that?

Turn the page to find out.

Electrons hop back and forth between a balloon and hair, making your hair stand up.

Electrons move in batteries, making toy planes fly.

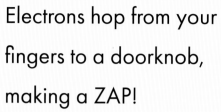

Electrons hop from your fingers to a doorknob, making a ZAP!

Electrons move in wires to power a toaster.

How to say science words

atom (AA-tum)

electrical energy (i-LEK-tri-kuhl E-nuhr-jee)

electricity (i-lek-TRI-suh-tee)

electron (i-LEK-trahn)

energy (E-nuhr-jee)

force (FAWRS)

location (loh-KAY-shun)

shape (SHAYP)

work (WERK)

What questions do you have about

ELECTRICITY?

Learn More Real Science!

Complete science curricula from Real Science-4-Kids

Focus On Series

Unit study for elementary and middle school levels

Chemistry
Biology
Physics
Geology
Astronomy

Exploring Science Series

Graded series for levels K–8. Each book contains 4 chapters of:

Chemistry
Biology
Physics
Geology
Astronomy

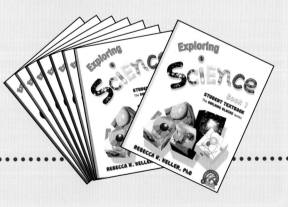